Chakra Coloring

Relax your body and quiet your mind. Breathe into each chakra as you color in order to channel more confidence, creativity and joy into your life.

Introduction

According to ancient meditation practices, human life is experienced in the physical body and also in a parallel "subtle body" where matter and consciousness meet. The subtle body consists of seven concentrated energy centers called Chakras or "wheels." These are located along the spine, through the neck and crown of the head. The function of the chakras is to draw in, incorporate and emanate energy in order to maintain optimal spiritual, mental, emotional and physical health. When a chakra is blocked or imbalanced, well-being is negatively effected so it is essential that our seven main chakras stay open, aligned, and fluid.

When the chakras are in balance we connect with ourselves more fully and live in harmony. This creates true holistic healing to decrease stress and keep us healthy, happy and vibrant. Enjoy, discover and investigate the chakras for yourself.

Root Chakra

The first chakra or Root *"Muladhara"* Chakra is located at the base of the spine and lays the foundation on which we build our lives.

This Power Base Governs:
Security, stability, survival and personal control of life

Balancing this Chakra Assists:
Trusting in life, feeling safe, centered, grounded, strong, supported

Primary Color: Red

Sound: Lam

Meditation:
"Security and stability in life allow me to move with confidence and connection to who I am."

Relax and breathe into the area at the base of the spine as you color these Root Chakra pages

Root Chakra

Root Chakra

Root Chakra

Sacral Chakra

The second chakra or Sacral *"Svadhisthana"* Chakra is located slightly below the navel.

This Creative & Sexual Center Governs:
Physical vitality, desire and passion

Balancing this Chakra Assists:
Sensuality, pleasure, creativity, optimism, emotional stability, spontaneity

Primary Color: Orange

Sound: Vam

Meditation:
*"Creative and sexual energy runs through me.
I embrace pleasure and abundance."*

Relax and breathe into the area slightly below the navel as you color the Sacral Chakra pages

Sacral Chakra

Sacral Chakra

Sacral Chakra

Solar Plexus Chakra

The third or Solar Plexus "Manipura" Chakra is located in the area two inches above the navel.

This Power Center Governs:
Personal power, confidence and drive

Balancing this Chakra Assists:
Sense of purpose, self-esteem, assertiveness, motivation, charisma, ambition to pursue goals

Primary Color: Yellow

Sound: Ram

Meditation:
"I honor the power within me. I respect myself and can manifest easily and gracefully."

Relax and breathe into the area above the navel as you color the Solar Plexus Chakra pages

Solar Plexus Chakra

Solar Plexus Chakra

Solar Plexus Chakra

Heart Chakra

The fourth chakra or Heart "Anahata" Chakra
is located at the center of the chest

This Love Center Governs:
Compassion, trust, self-love and love
for the world

Balancing this Chakra Assists:
The ability to give and receive love, acceptance,
empathy, healing

Primary Color: Green

Sound: Yam

Meditation:
*"I am loved. I give love effortlessly. I am a source of
healing in the world."*

Relax and breathe into the center of the chest as you color the Heart Chakra pages

Heart Chakra

Heart Chakra

Heart Chakra

Throat Chakra

The fifth chakra or Throat "Vishuddha" Chakra is located a the center of the throat.

This Expression Center Governs:
Personal power and the ability to speak from truth, communicate needs and react with balance

Balancing this Chakra Assists:
Self-expression, authenticity, expression of creativity

Primary Color: Blue

Sound: Ham

Meditation:
"I know my truth. I express myself clearly and freely with grace and ease."

Relax and breathe into the the Throat Chakra as you color these pages

Throat Chakra

Throat Chakra

Throat Chakra

Third Eye Chakra

The sixth chakra or Third Eye "Ajna" Chakra is located in the center of the forehead.

This Perception Center Governs:
Wisdom and intuitive ability

Balancing this Chakra Assists:
Insight, awareness, differentiating truth from illusion, focus, clear thoughts and vision, seeing beyond the physical

Primary Color: Indigo

Sound: Sham

Meditation:
"I trust my intuition and follow my inner guidance. I am on a path towards my deepest purpose."

Relax and breathe into the center of the forehead as you color the Third Eye Chakra pages

Third Eye Chakra

Third Eye Chakra

Third Eye Chakra

Crown Chakra

The seventh chakra or Crown "Sahasrara"
Chakra is located at the top of the head.

This Spiritual Center Governs:
States of higher consciousness and divine connection

Balancing this Chakra Assists:
Connection to a higher purpose, wise understanding,
spiritual intelligence, living in the present, bliss

Primary Color: Violet

Sound: Om

Meditation:
*"I am at peace in this moment. I am one with my higher
self and the divine. I trust myself and the flow of life."*

Relax and breathe into the top of the head as you color the Crown Chakra pages

Crown Chakra

Crown Chakra

Crown Chakra

Notes:

Made in the USA
Middletown, DE
03 January 2020